FHA Loans for Borrowers with Low Credit or Past Credit Issues

How to Get Approved with FHA Even with Late Payments, Collections, or a Low Credit Score

By Joseph G. Correa

Licensed Mortgage Broker, Finibi Mortgage

Copyright & Legal Notice

Published by Live Stronger Faster

First Edition, 2026

Table of Contents

Foreword

For millions of Americans, the dream of homeownership feels just out of reach—not because they lack the desire to own a home, but because at some point in their financial journey, life happened. Missed payments, medical bills, job loss, divorce, business setbacks, collections, charge-offs, or a credit score that doesn't reflect who they are today can quietly close doors that once felt open. The traditional mortgage world often treats credit reports as final verdicts rather than snapshots in time, and borrowers are too often judged by past mistakes instead of present stability. This book exists because that judgment is incomplete—and because FHA loans were created to serve borrowers exactly like this.

The Federal Housing Administration did not design its loan programs for perfect borrowers. FHA was created to expand access to homeownership, to provide opportunity during economic recovery, and to offer a path forward for families who might otherwise be excluded from the housing market. Yet despite FHA's mission, confusion, misinformation, and outdated advice still prevent many borrowers with low credit or past credit challenges from realizing that they may already qualify—or be far closer to qualifying than they've been led to believe. This book is written to replace fear with clarity, and myths with facts, so borrowers can finally understand how FHA underwriting actually works.

Too often, borrowers are told “no” by a bank, an online lender, or a loan officer who does not fully understand FHA guidelines, overlays, or compensating factors. That single rejection becomes internalized as a permanent barrier, even when the truth is far more flexible. FHA does not require perfect credit. FHA does not demand spotless financial history. FHA looks at patterns, recovery, and the total picture of a borrower’s ability to manage a mortgage moving forward. This book is designed to help borrowers see that picture clearly, without shame, confusion, or guesswork.

This series was written with one goal in mind: to educate borrowers so they can advocate for themselves. Knowledge changes outcomes. When borrowers understand how FHA evaluates late payments, collections, charge-offs, bankruptcies, foreclosures, credit scores, debt ratios, income stability, and compensating factors, they stop approaching the mortgage process from a position of fear and start approaching it with strategy. This book does not promise shortcuts or loopholes. Instead, it provides honest, practical guidance grounded in real underwriting standards and real-world lending experience. Book 3 focuses specifically on borrowers with low credit or past credit issues because this group is the most underserved, misunderstood, and discouraged in the housing market. These borrowers are often responsible, hardworking individuals who experienced setbacks—not irresponsibility. FHA recognizes this reality, and its guidelines reflect a more human approach to lending. By understanding those guidelines, borrowers can take meaningful steps to position themselves for approval, sometimes faster than they ever imagined possible.

Throughout this book, readers will learn that credit scores are only one part of the equation. FHA allows approvals with lower scores than conventional loans, but more importantly, FHA evaluates recent credit behavior, payment history, and the borrower's ability to recover from past events. A borrower with collections but clean recent payment history may be viewed more favorably than someone with a higher score but ongoing late payments. This distinction is critical, and it is rarely explained clearly outside of professional underwriting conversations. This book brings that conversation directly to the borrower.

Another purpose of this book is to remove the emotional weight many borrowers carry when they think about their credit. Shame is one of the most powerful obstacles to progress. Borrowers delay applying, asking questions, or seeking help because they assume they are not "good enough" yet. FHA lending does not operate on shame—it operates on documented facts, guidelines, and risk assessment. Once borrowers understand what matters and what does not, they can focus their energy on the actions that actually move the needle instead of stressing over outdated myths.

This book is also part of a larger series because FHA is not just a loan—it is a tool. Used correctly, FHA loans can help borrowers buy their first home, recover financially, refinance strategically, build equity, access cash responsibly, and even create long-term wealth. Borrowers with past credit challenges are not excluded from these opportunities. In many cases, FHA is the very bridge that allows them to transition from financial recovery to financial growth. This book represents one step in that broader journey.

The FHA Homeownership & Wealth Series was designed to meet borrowers where they are, not where someone else thinks they should be. Each book addresses a specific situation, and Book 3 speaks directly to those who feel like their credit history defines them. It does not. What defines borrowers is their willingness to learn, prepare, and take action. FHA lending rewards preparation and stability, not perfection, and this book shows readers exactly how to demonstrate both.

As you move through this book, you will gain a clearer understanding of how lenders view late payments, collections, charge-offs, judgments, bankruptcies, foreclosures, short sales, and credit rebuilding timelines. You will learn what matters most today, what underwriters look for tomorrow, and how to position yourself for long-term success—not just loan approval. The goal is not simply to get approved, but to do so confidently, responsibly, and sustainably.

This book is written for borrowers, but it is also written with respect for the professionals involved in the mortgage process. FHA guidelines are detailed for a reason: they balance access with responsibility. By learning how those guidelines work, borrowers become better partners in the lending process. They ask better questions, make better decisions, and avoid unnecessary delays or denials. Empowered borrowers create smoother transactions and better outcomes for everyone involved.

Homeownership is more than a purchase—it is stability, control, and opportunity. For borrowers with past credit challenges, it is often also a statement of resilience. FHA loans make that statement possible when borrowers understand how to use them correctly. This book is not about rewriting the past; it is about building the future with clarity, intention, and confidence. If you are reading this book because you were told you could not qualify, because your credit score worries you, or because past financial mistakes still feel heavy, know this: FHA was designed with you in mind. With the right knowledge and preparation, homeownership may be closer than you think. This book is your guide to understanding what is possible—and how to take the next step forward.

Welcome to Book 3 of the FHA Homeownership & Wealth Series. Your past does not disqualify you. Your future is still being written.

Chapter 1

Your Credit Score Is Not Your Story: How FHA Looks Beyond the Numbers

For many borrowers, the moment they think about buying a home, their mind goes straight to one number: their credit score. That number often feels like a final judgment, a label that determines whether homeownership is possible or permanently out of reach. Borrowers with low credit scores or past credit issues frequently assume they must "fix everything" before even thinking about an FHA loan. This belief is one of the most damaging myths in mortgage lending, because FHA does not view borrowers through a single number—it evaluates patterns, recovery, and overall risk in a much broader and more human way.

FHA lending was designed to account for real life. Job losses happen. Medical emergencies happen. Businesses fail and restart. Divorces disrupt finances. Economic downturns affect entire households at once. FHA understands that credit reports are historical documents, not personality tests or moral evaluations. What matters most to FHA is not whether something went wrong in the past, but whether the borrower has demonstrated the ability to manage obligations moving forward. This philosophy is the foundation of FHA underwriting, and it is why borrowers with lower credit scores often qualify when they least expect it.

Unlike conventional loans, which rely heavily on automated systems that prioritize credit scores and rigid risk thresholds, FHA underwriting places greater emphasis on compensating factors. These include stable income, manageable debt, documented recovery from past credit events, consistent rent history, savings behavior, and the absence of new derogatory credit. A borrower with a 580 credit score but stable income and clean recent payment history may be a stronger FHA candidate than a borrower with a 680 score who continues to miss payments. FHA looks at behavior over time, not just outcomes.

One of the most misunderstood aspects of FHA loans is how late payments are evaluated. FHA does not automatically disqualify borrowers for late payments on credit cards, auto loans, or even previous mortgages. What matters is when the late payments occurred, how frequent they were, and whether there is a reasonable explanation followed by recovery. Late payments from two or three years ago are viewed very differently than late payments within the past 12 months. FHA underwriters are trained to identify patterns of improvement, not punish historical hardship. Collections and charge-offs are another major source of fear for borrowers. Many assume that all collections must be paid before applying for an FHA loan. This is not true. FHA does not require all collections to be paid, and in many cases, paying them can actually harm a borrower's profile by reducing available cash or triggering new credit activity. Instead, FHA applies specific rules to how collections are counted in debt-to-income calculations, depending on the balance and type of account. Understanding these rules can mean the difference between approval and denial, and they are often misunderstood by borrowers and loan officers alike.

Bankruptcies and foreclosures, while serious credit events, are not permanent barriers under FHA guidelines. FHA allows borrowers to qualify after bankruptcy and foreclosure once specific waiting periods are met and recovery is documented. More importantly, FHA evaluates how borrowers handled credit after those events. A borrower who rebuilt responsibly after bankruptcy may be viewed more favorably than someone who never filed bankruptcy but continues to struggle with late payments. FHA focuses on sustainability, not stigma.

Another critical concept in FHA lending is the idea of layered risk. No single weakness automatically disqualifies a borrower. Instead, underwriters assess how multiple factors interact. A lower credit score may be offset by a lower loan amount, higher down payment, strong income stability, or significant reserves. Conversely, multiple risk factors layered together—such as low credit, high debt, and unstable income—may require additional preparation. This layered approach allows FHA to serve a wider range of borrowers while still managing risk responsibly.

Debt-to-income ratios also play a major role in FHA approvals, but they are often misunderstood. FHA allows higher debt ratios than many conventional programs, especially when borrowers demonstrate compensating factors. A borrower with higher monthly obligations may still qualify if their income is stable, their housing payment is reasonable, and their overall financial picture supports long-term repayment. FHA does not expect borrowers to be debt-free—it expects them to be capable.

Perhaps the most empowering truth about FHA loans is that borrowers can influence their approval outcomes more than they realize. Strategic timing, targeted credit improvement, documentation, and lender selection all matter. A borrower who understands FHA guidelines can take intentional steps to strengthen their profile without chasing perfection. This chapter exists to shift borrowers from fear-based assumptions to strategy-based decisions.

The purpose of this book is not to promise approval to

everyone, but to provide clarity. When borrowers understand how FHA actually works, they stop guessing and start planning. They stop assuming rejection and start preparing for success. FHA lending is not about being flawless—it is about being ready. And readiness is something borrowers can build.

From 547 to the Front Door: A Numbers-Based FHA Comeback

When Maria first checked her credit score, it read 547. She stared at the number on her phone, convinced that homeownership was impossible. Five years earlier, she had gone through a divorce that left her with late payments, a charged-off credit card, and a small medical collection. She assumed she needed years of perfect credit before even thinking about buying a home. What she didn't realize was that FHA was already looking at her situation very differently.

Maria earned $5,000 per month before taxes from her full-time job. Her monthly debts included a $350 car payment, $75 in minimum credit card payments, and a $120 student loan payment, totaling $545 per month. She paid $1,600 in rent every month and had not missed a rent payment in over two years. Despite her low credit score, her recent payment history was clean, and her income was stable.

When Maria spoke with an FHA-focused lender, they

explained how FHA would evaluate her numbers. Using FHA guidelines, the lender estimated a target housing payment of around 31% of her gross monthly income. Thirty-one percent of $5,000 equals $1,550. This meant that her potential FHA mortgage payment could be close to what she was already paying in rent.

Next, they looked at her debt-to-income ratio. Her existing monthly debt of $545 plus a projected FHA mortgage payment of $1,550 resulted in total monthly obligations of $2,095. Dividing $2,095 by her $5,000 monthly income resulted in a back-end debt ratio of approximately 41.9%. This fell well within FHA's allowable range, especially given her stable income and clean recent payment history.

Maria also had one collection account with a balance of $2,000. FHA rules required the lender to include either 5% of the collection balance or a documented payment plan in her debt calculations. Five percent of $2,000 is $100. Even after adding $100 to her monthly debt total, her revised obligations became $2,195 per month. Dividing $2,195 by $5,000 resulted in a debt ratio of 43.9%, still acceptable under FHA guidelines.

The lender explained that Maria did not need to pay off the collection to qualify. In fact, keeping her savings intact for closing costs was more important. Maria had saved $9,000 over time, enough to cover her FHA down payment and most of her closing costs. With a minimum 3.5% down payment on a $250,000 home, her required down payment was $8,750. The numbers worked. Over the next two months, Maria focused on maintaining her payment history and avoiding new credit inquiries. Her credit score increased slightly to 564, but more importantly, her profile showed consistency and recovery. When her FHA loan was submitted for underwriting, the underwriter focused on her income stability, rent history, savings, and clean recent credit behavior. Her past issues were acknowledged, but they were no longer defining.

Maria was approved for her FHA loan at a monthly payment slightly below her rent. The math told a story her credit score alone never could. A borrower with a 547 score became a homeowner not by fixing the past, but by proving readiness for the future. FHA didn't ignore her credit history—it understood it in context.

That is the power of knowing how FHA lending really works.

Chapter 2

Timing Is Everything: How Recent Credit Behavior Can Make or Break an FHA Approval

One of the most misunderstood aspects of FHA lending is not credit score, collections, or past financial hardship—it is timing. Borrowers often assume that if something negative appears on their credit report, it carries equal weight forever. In reality, FHA underwriting places tremendous emphasis on *when* credit events occurred and *what happened afterward.* The difference between denial and approval often has less to do with how bad something was and more to do with how long ago it happened and what the borrower did next.

FHA underwriting is built on the idea that people recover. The system is designed to identify borrowers who have stabilized, not to punish those who stumbled. As a result, FHA underwriters focus heavily on the most recent 12 to 24 months of credit behavior. This period tells the clearest story about whether a borrower is ready to take on the responsibility of a mortgage payment. Even borrowers with serious past credit issues can qualify if their recent history shows consistency, responsibility, and improvement. Late payments are one of the most common concerns for FHA borrowers. A single late payment does not automatically disqualify a borrower, and even multiple late payments may be acceptable depending on timing and explanation. FHA underwriters look for patterns rather than isolated incidents. A borrower who experienced late payments during a job loss two years ago but has paid all obligations on time since returning to work is viewed far differently than a borrower who missed payments within the last six months. Recent behavior matters most because it reflects current financial habits.

The same principle applies to collections, charge-offs, and even judgments. FHA does not require perfection, but it does require stabilization. A borrower with old collections who has not added new derogatory accounts in the past year is often viewed as lower risk than someone with fewer collections but ongoing credit issues. FHA underwriters ask a simple but powerful question: has this borrower stopped the financial bleeding and established control over their obligations?

New credit activity is another timing-related factor that borrowers frequently underestimate. Opening new credit accounts, financing vehicles, or increasing credit card balances shortly before applying for an FHA loan can weaken an otherwise solid application. FHA underwriters prefer to see calm, predictable financial behavior leading up to approval.

Stability signals readiness. Sudden changes signal risk, even when credit scores increase slightly as a result.

Waiting periods after major credit events are another area where timing is crucial. FHA allows borrowers to qualify after bankruptcy, foreclosure, deed-in-lieu, and short sale, but only after specific waiting periods have passed. These waiting periods exist not as punishment, but as proof-of-recovery windows. FHA wants to see that borrowers can maintain stable housing, manage credit responsibly, and avoid repeating past mistakes. Borrowers who use these waiting periods wisely often qualify immediately once the clock runs out.

Income stability also intersects with credit timing. FHA underwriting looks more favorably on borrowers who have been in the same line of work or employment for at least two years. A borrower with improving credit and stable income sends a powerful signal to underwriters. Even if income fluctuates, such as with hourly or overtime pay, FHA allows averages when documentation supports consistency. Timing of income changes, raises, or job transitions can significantly affect approval outcomes.

Another overlooked factor is rental history. FHA places strong value on demonstrated housing payment performance. A borrower who has paid rent on time for the past 12 months, especially when rent is equal to or higher than the proposed mortgage payment, presents a compelling case. In many situations, consistent rent payments carry more weight than a credit score alone. Timing matters here as well—recent, verifiable rent history is far more impactful than older housing records.

The most strategic FHA borrowers understand that approval is often about preparation rather than repair. They avoid applying too early, when recent credit behavior could raise concerns, and instead wait until their profile tells a stronger story. This does not mean waiting years—it often means waiting months. A borrower who delays application by three to six months to establish clean payment history can dramatically change the outcome of their loan.

This chapter exists to reframe how borrowers think about time. FHA does not demand that borrowers erase the past. It asks them to demonstrate readiness in the present. When borrowers understand this, they stop reacting emotionally to their credit reports and start planning strategically. Timing is not passive—it is something borrowers can control. Knowing when to apply is just as important as knowing how.

Six Months That Changed Everything: An FHA Timing Turnaround

When Daniel first reached out to an FHA lender, his credit score was 562. He had two late credit card payments from eight months earlier, a small collection, and a recently financed vehicle. His income was solid—$6,200 per month—but his loan application was denied due to recent credit activity and timing concerns. The denial felt personal, but the math told a different story.

Daniel's proposed FHA mortgage payment was estimated at $1,750 per month. His existing debts included a $425 car payment, $90 in minimum credit card payments, and $85 in student loans, totaling $600 per month. Adding the proposed housing payment brought his total monthly obligations to $2,350. Dividing $2,350 by his $6,200 monthly income resulted in a debt-to-income ratio of approximately 37.9%, well within FHA limits. On paper, the numbers worked.

The issue was timing. Daniel had opened his auto loan just three months earlier and had missed two credit card payments within the past year. The underwriter explained that while the math supported approval, the recent credit behavior created uncertainty. The solution was not to improve the numbers, but to let time do its work. Daniel was advised to make all payments on time, avoid new credit, and reduce his credit card balances slightly. Over the next six months, he followed the plan precisely. His credit score increased modestly to 585, but more importantly, his recent payment history became spotless. His credit profile calmed.

When Daniel reapplied six months later, the numbers were nearly identical. His income remained $6,200 per month. His debts dropped slightly to $560 after paying down cards. His total obligations with the FHA payment were now $2,310, resulting in a debt ratio of approximately 37.3%. The math had barely changed—but the story had.

This time, the underwriter focused on Daniel's six months of clean payment history following prior issues. The late payments were now over a year old. The auto loan was seasoned. The risk profile improved without drastic changes. Daniel was approved for his FHA loan with terms similar to the original estimate.

Six months did not erase Daniel's past—but it proved his present. FHA lending rewarded timing, patience, and consistency. The numbers were always strong enough. The story simply needed time to catch up.

That is the power of understanding FHA timing.

Chapter 3

The Approval Equation: How FHA Compensating Factors Turn "Almost" Into "Approved"

Many FHA borrowers believe approval is a simple pass-or-fail test, as though a computer reviews their application and delivers a final verdict with no room for interpretation. In reality, FHA approvals are the result of an equation made up of multiple variables, and compensating factors are often the elements that tip the balance. Understanding these factors allows borrowers to shift their mindset from hoping for approval to actively building it.

FHA underwriting is designed to evaluate overall risk, not individual imperfections. When one part of a borrower's profile is weaker, other strengths can offset that weakness. These strengths are known as compensating factors. They do not erase risk, but they demonstrate the borrower's ability to manage it. For borrowers with low credit scores or past credit issues, compensating factors often matter more than the score itself.

Income stability is one of the strongest compensating factors in FHA lending. A borrower who has remained in the same line of work for several years demonstrates predictability, even if their credit history includes setbacks. FHA values stable employment because it supports long-term repayment. Even borrowers with variable income, such as hourly workers or those receiving overtime, may qualify when income is documented and averaged correctly. Consistency outweighs perfection.

Cash reserves also play a powerful role in the approval equation. FHA does not require large reserves for most owner-occupied purchases, but having savings after closing sends a strong signal to underwriters. Reserves demonstrate the borrower's ability to absorb unexpected expenses without falling behind on mortgage payments. For borrowers with weaker credit, even one to three months of reserves can materially strengthen the file.

Housing payment history is another compensating factor that FHA underwriters take seriously. A borrower who has paid rent on time for 12 months, especially when rent is similar to or higher than the proposed mortgage payment, proves real-world ability to handle housing costs. This history often carries more weight than revolving credit behavior because it directly mirrors the responsibility of homeownership.

Lower loan amounts and conservative payment structures can also offset credit weaknesses. Borrowers who choose homes well within their budget rather than stretching to maximum approval limits present lower risk. FHA underwriters recognize this restraint. A borrower who qualifies for a higher amount but opts for a smaller, more affordable payment strengthens their profile through prudence.

Debt structure matters as much as debt totals. FHA allows higher debt-to-income ratios, but the composition of that debt matters. Installment debt with fixed payments is often viewed more favorably than high revolving balances that fluctuate. Borrowers who reduce credit card utilization, even modestly, often improve both their credit profile and underwriting risk simultaneously.

Lender overlays introduce another layer of complexity. While FHA sets baseline guidelines, lenders may impose stricter requirements. Borrowers with low credit often receive conflicting information because different lenders apply different overlays. Understanding this distinction is critical. A denial from one lender does not mean FHA denial—it often means overlay denial. Borrowers who understand this seek lenders that underwrite to true FHA standards rather than unnecessarily conservative interpretations.

Manual underwriting is another tool that allows FHA loans to be approved when automated systems hesitate. Manual underwriting evaluates the full financial picture and gives compensating factors greater weight. Borrowers with strong rent history, stable income, and documented recovery often succeed through manual underwriting when automated systems produce cautionary results. This path requires documentation and patience, but it exists for a reason.

The FHA approval equation is not static. Borrowers can influence it through intentional decisions. Saving additional funds, waiting to apply, choosing a lower-priced home, paying down small balances, or documenting income more thoroughly can all strengthen compensating factors. These adjustments do not require perfection—they require awareness.

This chapter exists to show borrowers that approval is not luck. It is built. FHA loans reward preparation, stability, and strategy. When borrowers understand compensating factors, they stop feeling powerless and start participating actively in their approval outcome. FHA underwriting is not a mystery—it is a system, and systems can be navigated.

The Extra Margin: How Compensating Factors Sealed an FHA Approval

Anthony's credit score was 575. He had a few late payments from two years earlier and one charged-off credit card with a balance of $1,800. His income was steady at $4,800 per month, and he had been employed with the same company for over five years. Despite his credit history, he wanted to buy a modest home priced at $235,000.

Anthony planned to put down the FHA minimum of 3.5%, which amounted to $8,225. His estimated monthly FHA mortgage payment, including taxes, insurance, and mortgage insurance, came to approximately $1,620. His existing monthly debts included a $290 car payment and $95 in minimum credit card payments, totaling $385.

Adding the housing payment to his debts resulted in total monthly obligations of $2,005. Dividing $2,005 by his $4,800 income produced a debt-to-income ratio of approximately 41.8%. This ratio was within FHA limits, but the underwriter still needed reassurance due to Anthony's low credit score.

Anthony had one key advantage: reserves. After closing costs, he would still have $6,500 in savings. This represented approximately four months of his proposed mortgage payment. Additionally, Anthony had paid $1,650 in rent every month for over two years without a single late payment. His rent history closely matched his proposed FHA payment.

The underwriter evaluated Anthony's compensating factors together. His long-term employment demonstrated stability. His reserves showed financial cushioning. His rent history proved real-world housing responsibility. His loan amount was conservative relative to income, and his debt ratio was manageable.

Even though the charged-off account remained unpaid, FHA guidelines allowed it to remain as-is. The underwriter added a small assumed payment to the debt calculation, but Anthony's ratios still worked. The strength of his compensating factors outweighed the weakness of his credit score.

Anthony's FHA loan was approved. The math alone supported the loan, but the compensating factors told the story. FHA did not ignore risk—it balanced it. The approval was not accidental. It was built.

That is the approval equation in action.

Chapter 4

Collections, Charge-Offs, and the Truth About Unpaid Debt in FHA Loans

Few things intimidate FHA borrowers more than seeing collections and charge-offs on their credit report. These accounts often feel like permanent stains—evidence of failure that borrowers assume must be erased before a lender will ever say yes. As a result, many borrowers delay applying for an FHA loan or rush to pay off old debts without understanding the consequences. The reality is far more nuanced. FHA does not view unpaid debt as an automatic disqualifier. Instead, it evaluates how that debt affects cash flow, risk, and future stability.

FHA guidelines recognize a simple truth: unpaid debt exists for many borrowers, especially those who experienced financial hardship. Medical bills, utility balances, old credit cards, and personal loans frequently end up in collections during periods of instability. FHA does not require borrowers to have a clean credit report. It requires borrowers to demonstrate that past issues are not continuing patterns. This distinction changes everything. One of the most important misconceptions is the belief that all collections must be paid off before closing. FHA does not impose this rule. In fact, paying off collections can sometimes weaken a borrower's profile by draining savings or triggering new credit activity. FHA focuses less on whether a collection exists and more on how it is accounted for in the debt-to-income calculation and whether the borrower has established financial control since the account went delinquent.

For non-medical collections, FHA applies a standardized approach. If the total outstanding balance of non-medical collections exceeds a certain threshold, underwriters must include a calculated monthly obligation in the borrower's debt ratios. This obligation is not based on an actual payment unless a payment agreement exists. Instead, FHA uses an assumed percentage of the outstanding balance to estimate risk. This approach allows borrowers to qualify without paying off old debts while still acknowledging their impact on affordability.

Medical collections are treated differently. FHA does not require a payment calculation for medical collections, regardless of balance. This distinction reflects the understanding that medical debt often arises unexpectedly and does not reflect poor financial management. Borrowers with large medical collections are often relieved to learn that these accounts may not affect their FHA approval at all.

Charge-offs are another area of confusion. A charged-off account means the creditor has written off the debt for accounting purposes, not that the borrower is required to resolve it for FHA approval. FHA does not require charged-off accounts to be paid. Instead, underwriters evaluate when the charge-off occurred and whether the borrower continued responsible credit behavior afterward. Old charge-offs followed by clean payment history are often viewed as resolved risk.

Judgments and liens are treated more seriously, but they are not always deal-breakers. FHA requires that judgments be addressed, either through payoff or documented payment plans. What matters most is predictability. An underwriter wants to know exactly how a judgment affects monthly obligations and whether the borrower can manage it alongside a mortgage payment. When properly structured, payment plans often allow borrowers to move forward without delaying homeownership for years.

Another overlooked factor is borrower intent. FHA underwriting distinguishes between unresolved chaos and controlled recovery. A borrower with old collections who has avoided new credit problems demonstrates stabilization. A borrower actively disputing every account or repeatedly opening new credit lines signals ongoing risk. FHA favors calm, predictable financial behavior leading up to approval. Borrowers sometimes attempt to clean up their credit aggressively right before applying, paying off accounts without strategy. This can reduce cash reserves, increase utilization temporarily, or create documentation issues. FHA underwriting prefers intentional, documented decisions over reactive cleanup. In many cases, doing nothing is the correct strategy—especially when collections are old and cash is better used for closing costs and reserves.

Understanding how FHA treats unpaid debt allows borrowers to make informed choices. Instead of guessing or assuming denial, borrowers can evaluate how collections and charge-offs affect their ratios and risk profile. FHA loans are not about erasing the past. They are about proving that the past no longer controls the present.

This chapter exists to replace fear with facts. Collections do not disqualify borrowers. Ignorance of how they are evaluated does. When borrowers understand the rules, unpaid debt becomes a manageable variable—not a stopping point.

The $12,000 Collection That Didn't Stop the Loan

Tanya believed her FHA dreams were over when she added up her collections. Between an old credit card, a utility bill, and a personal loan, her non-medical collections totaled $12,000.

Her credit score was 571, and she assumed no lender would look past that number. What Tanya didn't understand was how FHA would actually calculate her risk.

Tanya earned $5,400 per month from her salaried job and had been employed with the same company for over three years. She wanted to purchase a $245,000 home using FHA financing. Her estimated monthly FHA mortgage payment, including taxes, insurance, and mortgage insurance, was $1,690.

Her existing monthly debts included a $310 car payment and $95 in minimum credit card payments, totaling $405. FHA guidelines required the lender to include an assumed payment for her non-medical collections. Using FHA's standard calculation, 5 percent of her $12,000 collection balance resulted in an assumed monthly obligation of $600.

Adding the collection calculation to her existing debts brought her total monthly non-housing obligations to $1,005. When combined with her proposed mortgage payment of $1,690, Tanya's total monthly obligations equaled $2,695. Dividing $2,695 by her $5,400 monthly income resulted in a debt-to-income ratio of approximately 49.9 percent.

At first glance, this number appeared high. However, the underwriter evaluated Tanya's full profile. She had paid

$1,700 in rent on time for over two years. Her income was stable. Her collections were over three years old. She had $7,200 in savings after closing, providing over four months of housing reserves. The lender explored an alternative strategy. Tanya agreed to set up a payment plan on one collection for $150 per month. FHA allowed the actual payment to replace the assumed calculation. Her revised monthly obligations dropped significantly. With the $150 payment included, her total non-housing debt fell to $555. Adding her FHA payment resulted in total obligations of $2,245.

Dividing $2,245 by $5,400 produced a new debt ratio of approximately 41.6 percent. With strong compensating factors, the underwriter approved the loan.

Tanya did not pay off $12,000 in debt. She structured it intelligently. The math changed. The outcome changed. FHA did what it was designed to do—look beyond the fear and focus on feasibility.

That is the real truth about collections and FHA loans.

Chapter 5

When the Computer Says No: How Manual Underwriting Opens the Door to FHA Approval

For many borrowers with low credit or past credit challenges, the most discouraging moment in the mortgage process comes when an automated system delivers a quick denial. The decision often feels final, as though a machine has weighed the borrower's worthiness and issued a verdict with no appeal. In FHA lending, however, automated underwriting is only the first step, not the last. Manual underwriting exists specifically to ensure that capable borrowers are not excluded simply because their financial story does not fit neatly into a formula.

FHA manual underwriting allows a human underwriter to evaluate the full financial picture rather than relying solely on algorithmic risk models. This process was created because FHA recognizes that recovery, stability, and responsibility cannot always be captured by automated systems. Borrowers with limited credit history, recent recovery from hardship, or unique financial patterns often benefit from manual review when automated results are inconclusive or negative. One of the most important distinctions between automated and manual underwriting is how compensating factors are weighted. Automated systems tend to penalize lower credit scores and recent credit events heavily. Manual underwriting allows underwriters to emphasize strengths such as stable employment, consistent rent history, cash reserves, and documented explanations for past credit issues. For borrowers who have turned a corner financially, manual underwriting often reveals a much stronger profile than automated results suggest.

Manual underwriting also applies different debt-to-income thresholds. While automated approvals may allow higher ratios, manual underwriting typically requires more conservative limits unless strong compensating factors are present. This structure encourages responsible borrowing while still offering flexibility. Borrowers who understand these thresholds can prepare intentionally by managing debts, saving reserves, and selecting affordable home prices.

Documentation plays a central role in manual underwriting. Borrowers must demonstrate stability through verified income, housing payment history, and explanations of past credit events. This is not meant to create barriers but to replace assumptions with clarity. A borrower who can clearly show how and why a financial hardship occurred—and how it was resolved—often gains credibility in the eyes of an underwriter.

Rental history becomes especially powerful in manual underwriting cases. FHA underwriters place significant value on a borrower's ability to make consistent housing payments. Twelve months of on-time rent payments can significantly strengthen a manually underwritten file, particularly when rent is comparable to the proposed mortgage payment. This real-world proof often outweighs weaknesses in revolving credit.

Another key element of manual underwriting is income reliability. FHA looks for stable or increasing income, even if it comes from hourly wages, overtime, or multiple sources. Consistency matters more than complexity. Borrowers who document their income thoroughly often find that manual underwriting works in their favor, especially when their earnings comfortably support the proposed housing payment.

Lender selection is critical when manual underwriting is needed. Not all lenders offer manual underwriting, and many apply overlays that restrict its use. Borrowers who receive denials often assume FHA itself has said no, when in reality, the lender simply does not allow manual reviews. Choosing a lender experienced in true FHA underwriting can be the difference between denial and approval.

Manual underwriting is not a loophole. It is a structured, guideline-driven process designed to evaluate borrowers fairly. It rewards preparation, honesty, and stability. Borrowers who understand this pathway stop fearing automated decisions and start building files that tell a clear, credible story.

This chapter exists to remind borrowers that a "no" from a computer is not the end of the road. FHA lending was built to include human judgment for a reason. When borrowers understand how manual underwriting works, they regain control over their approval outcome.

Approved Without an Algorithm: A Manual Underwriting Win

Lena's credit score was 556. She had two late payments from over a year ago and a small collection account that remained unpaid. When her loan application was run through an automated system, it returned an ineligible result. Lena assumed she was done. Instead, her lender recommended manual underwriting.

Lena earned $4,900 per month from her full-time job and had been employed in the same field for over four years. She wanted to purchase a $225,000 home using FHA financing.

Her estimated FHA mortgage payment, including taxes, insurance, and mortgage insurance, was $1,520.

Her existing monthly debts included a $280 car payment and $90 in credit card minimums, totaling $370. Adding her housing payment brought her total monthly obligations to $1,890. Dividing $1,890 by her $4,900 income resulted in a debt-to-income ratio of approximately 38.6 percent.

Manual underwriting guidelines required careful review of compensating factors. Lena had paid $1,500 in rent on time for over two years. She had $6,200 in savings after closing, representing over four months of mortgage payments. Her credit issues were tied to a short period of unemployment, followed by consistent recovery.

The underwriter reviewed Lena's explanation, documentation, and financial stability. The numbers supported sustainability. The rent history demonstrated reliability. The savings provided cushioning. The story made sense.

Lena's loan was approved through manual underwriting. The computer had said no, but the math—and the human review—said yes.

That is the power of manual underwriting when FHA guidelines are understood and applied correctly.

Chapter 6

The Credit Comeback Plan: How Strategic Rebuilding Sets the Stage for FHA Approval

For borrowers with low credit or past credit issues, rebuilding credit often feels overwhelming. Many assume they must achieve dramatic score increases before applying for an FHA loan, chasing perfection instead of progress. This mindset leads to frustration, wasted time, and poor financial decisions. FHA lending does not require flawless credit. It rewards strategic rebuilding that demonstrates stability, control, and readiness. Understanding how to rebuild credit with FHA in mind changes the entire process.

Credit rebuilding for FHA borrowers is not about doing everything—it is about doing the right things in the right order. FHA underwriters focus on recent behavior, payment consistency, and risk reduction. A borrower who improves their profile intentionally over three to six months often sees better results than someone who spends years attempting to clean every blemish from their report. FHA is forward-looking. It wants to see momentum. One of the most important rebuilding principles is payment discipline. On-time payments matter more than almost any other factor. Even with low credit scores, borrowers who demonstrate consistent, timely payments across all obligations send a strong signal to underwriters. FHA is less concerned with how many accounts exist and more concerned with how they are managed. One late payment during the rebuilding phase can undo months of progress.

Credit utilization also plays a critical role, but it must be handled carefully. Borrowers often rush to pay off all balances without understanding the impact on cash reserves. FHA underwriting values liquidity. Reducing utilization strategically—bringing balances below key thresholds—often improves credit scores while preserving cash. Small balance reductions can have outsized effects when done intentionally.

Opening new credit accounts is another area where borrowers make mistakes. While having active trade lines can help credit scores, opening multiple accounts shortly before applying for an FHA loan creates risk. FHA underwriters prefer seasoned credit. New accounts can lower average account age and introduce uncertainty. Rebuilding is about calming the credit profile, not energizing it.

Disputes and credit repair tactics also require caution. Disputing legitimate accounts can delay underwriting and raise questions about accuracy. FHA allows disputes in some cases, but underwriters often require disputed accounts to be resolved before closing. Borrowers who rebuild responsibly focus on behavior change rather than aggressive dispute strategies.

Another key element of credit rebuilding is documentation. FHA underwriters appreciate clarity. Borrowers who can explain past credit issues, demonstrate recovery, and show consistent income often strengthen their file significantly. Credit rebuilding is not just numerical—it is narrative. A clear, believable story paired with improving numbers creates confidence.

Timing is everything. Borrowers who rebuild for FHA should avoid major financial changes shortly before application. Stability matters more than speed. Waiting a few extra months to establish clean payment history often produces better results than applying prematurely. FHA underwriting rewards patience.

Perhaps the most empowering aspect of FHA-focused credit rebuilding is that it gives borrowers control. Instead of reacting emotionally to credit reports, borrowers can take deliberate steps that align with underwriting priorities. FHA loans are designed to support borrowers who learn, prepare, and recover. Rebuilding credit is not about erasing the past—it is about proving the future. This chapter exists to shift rebuilding from chaos to strategy. FHA approval does not require a perfect credit report. It requires a calm one. Borrowers who understand this stop chasing scores and start building stability. That is the credit comeback plan.

Three Cards, One Plan, and an FHA Approval

Marcus had a credit score of 552 and assumed homeownership was years away. He had three credit cards with balances totaling $4,800, all of which were maxed out. He earned $5,300 per month and paid $1,650 in rent. His credit report showed no recent late payments, but high utilization kept his score low.

Marcus wanted to buy a $240,000 home using FHA financing. His estimated FHA mortgage payment, including taxes, insurance, and mortgage insurance, was $1,670 per month. His existing debts included a $360 car payment and $120 in minimum credit card payments, totaling $480 per month.

Before rebuilding, Marcus's total monthly obligations with the FHA payment were $2,150. Dividing $2,150 by his $5,300 income resulted in a debt-to-income ratio of approximately 40.6 percent. The ratio worked, but the credit profile needed improvement.

Instead of paying off all debt, Marcus followed a strategic plan. He reduced each credit card balance to under 30 percent utilization using $2,200 from savings. His remaining balances totaled $2,600. His monthly credit card minimums dropped from $120 to $75, reducing his total monthly debts to $435.

After three months of on-time payments and no new credit activity, Marcus's credit score increased to 588. His updated total monthly obligations with the FHA payment became $2,105. Dividing $2,105 by $5,300 produced a new debt ratio of approximately 39.7 percent.

More importantly, Marcus still had $5,900 in savings after closing, representing over three months of housing reserves. His credit profile calmed. His numbers improved. His story made sense.

Marcus was approved for his FHA loan. He didn't eliminate debt—he controlled it. The math supported the move, and the strategy made the difference.

That is how credit rebuilding works when FHA guidelines lead the plan.

Chapter 7

Where You Apply Matters: How the Right FHA Lender Can Change Everything

Many FHA borrowers believe that approval depends entirely on their credit profile. When they are denied, they assume the denial reflects their financial readiness rather than the lender's internal rules. This misunderstanding causes unnecessary frustration and often delays homeownership by months or years. In reality, where a borrower applies can matter just as much as their income, credit, or debt. FHA sets national guidelines, but lenders decide how closely they follow them.

FHA guidelines establish the minimum standards for approval, but lenders are allowed to impose additional requirements known as overlays. These overlays are not FHA rules—they are lender preferences designed to reduce risk. One lender may require a higher credit score, lower debt ratios, or stricter documentation than FHA itself requires. Another lender may underwrite directly to FHA standards. Borrowers who do not understand this distinction often receive conflicting answers and assume the strictest interpretation is universal. This is especially impactful for borrowers with low credit or past credit issues. Overlays disproportionately affect these borrowers because they narrow the margin for approval. A borrower who meets FHA guidelines but falls short of a lender's overlay will receive a denial that feels final, even though FHA itself would allow the loan. Understanding this difference changes how borrowers interpret rejection. A denial does not always mean "not eligible." It often means "wrong lender."

Another critical factor is experience. FHA underwriting requires familiarity with nuanced rules around collections, compensating factors, manual underwriting, and documentation. Lenders that process a high volume of FHA loans are more comfortable navigating gray areas. Less experienced lenders may default to conservative decisions, even when guidelines allow flexibility. Borrowers benefit from working with lenders who specialize in FHA rather than treating it as an occasional product.

Communication also plays a role. A knowledgeable FHA lender does more than submit numbers to a system. They explain strategy, timing, and trade-offs. They help borrowers understand whether to apply now or wait, whether to pay down debt or retain reserves, and whether a manual underwrite is appropriate. This guidance can transform the same financial profile into a different outcome. The structure of the loan itself can influence approval. Some lenders guide borrowers toward conservative price points or payment structures that strengthen the file. Others push maximum approvals without regard for sustainability. FHA underwriting rewards restraint. Borrowers who work with lenders that prioritize long-term success often experience smoother approvals and better outcomes.

Borrowers should also understand that not all loan officers have equal authority or support. Some lenders restrict manual underwriting or discourage exceptions even when guidelines allow them. Others empower underwriters to evaluate full profiles. Choosing the right lender means choosing one that understands FHA's purpose, not just its paperwork.

This chapter exists to shift blame away from borrowers and toward understanding systems. FHA lending is not broken—but it is unevenly applied. Borrowers who learn how to select the right lender stop internalizing denial and start navigating strategically. Approval becomes a matter of alignment, not luck.

Homeownership should not depend on guessing which door to knock on. FHA loans were designed to expand access, and the right lender honors that mission. When borrowers understand this, they stop asking "What's wrong with me?" and start asking "Who can properly evaluate my file?" That question changes everything.

Denied Twice, Approved Once: The Power of the Right FHA Lender

Rachel had a credit score of 579 and a steady income of $5,100 per month. She had one old collection account and a few late payments from two years earlier. She applied with a large national bank and was denied due to a minimum credit score overlay of 620. She assumed FHA was off the table.

Rachel's proposed FHA mortgage payment was estimated at $1,620 per month on a $235,000 home. Her existing monthly debts included a $340 car payment and $85 in credit card minimums, totaling $425. Adding her housing payment resulted in total monthly obligations of $2,045. Dividing $2,045 by her $5,100 income produced a debt-to-income ratio of approximately 40.1 percent—well within FHA guidelines.

Despite the numbers working, the bank's overlay stopped the loan. Rachel applied with a second lender and received a similar response. Both lenders applied stricter internal rules that exceeded FHA requirements.

Finally, Rachel worked with an FHA-specialized lender who underwrote directly to FHA standards. The lender reviewed her full profile. Her income was stable. Her late payments were seasoned. Her rent history showed 18 months of on-time payments at $1,600 per month. She would retain $6,000 in savings after closing.

The math never changed. The lender did.

Rachel was approved for her FHA loan with the same numbers that had previously been rejected. The difference was not her credit score, income, or debt. It was alignment with a lender who understood FHA.

That is the power of applying in the right place.

Chapter 8

The Cash Illusion: Why Low Credit Does Not Mean You Need More Money to Buy with FHA

One of the most persistent myths facing borrowers with low credit or past credit issues is the belief that they must compensate with large amounts of cash. Many assume that a lower credit score automatically means a higher down payment, massive reserves, or tens of thousands of dollars at closing. This assumption stops qualified borrowers before they ever begin. FHA lending does not work this way. In fact, FHA was designed specifically to reduce cash barriers, not raise them.

FHA requires the same minimum down payment regardless of whether a borrower has a 580 score or a 740 score, as long as they meet the minimum threshold. Credit score affects risk assessment and interest rates, but it does not increase the required down payment under FHA guidelines. This is a critical distinction that many borrowers misunderstand. Low credit does not equal higher down payment in FHA lending.

Closing costs are another area where fear often outweighs facts. Borrowers with low credit frequently believe they must bring all closing costs out of pocket. FHA allows sellers to contribute toward closing costs, often up to a significant percentage of the purchase price. These contributions can dramatically reduce the amount of cash a borrower needs to bring to closing. Understanding how seller credits work allows borrowers to structure offers strategically rather than assuming financial defeat.

Gift funds are another powerful tool that FHA allows. Borrowers do not need to accumulate all funds themselves. FHA permits gift funds from approved sources, including family members, as long as documentation requirements are met. These funds can be used for down payment, closing costs, or both. Borrowers with low credit are often relieved to learn that accepting help does not weaken their application when done properly.

Reserves, while helpful, are often misunderstood. FHA does not require large reserves for most owner-occupied purchases. Having reserves strengthens a file, but lacking them does not automatically disqualify a borrower. Many borrowers confuse lender overlays with FHA rules, assuming that all lenders demand months of savings. FHA itself focuses more on affordability and sustainability than on cash accumulation.

Interest rates can affect monthly payments and long-term cost, but they do not change minimum cash requirements. Borrowers with lower credit scores may pay slightly higher rates, but FHA mortgage insurance and flexible guidelines often offset this difference compared to conventional alternatives. FHA focuses on access first and optimization second. For many borrowers, buying sooner with FHA and refinancing later is a strategic path rather than a compromise.

Another overlooked factor is how cash decisions interact with underwriting strength. Draining savings to pay off old debts can weaken a file more than it strengthens it. FHA underwriting often prefers borrowers to retain liquidity rather than eliminate low-impact debts. Cash is a stabilizing factor. Using it strategically rather than emotionally improves outcomes.

Borrowers who understand FHA cash rules stop assuming they must "save more" before applying. Instead, they focus on structuring deals intelligently. Negotiating seller credits, using gift funds, choosing affordable homes, and working with FHA-experienced lenders often reduce cash requirements significantly. FHA lending rewards planning, not panic.

This chapter exists to dismantle the idea that low credit equals high cash. FHA was designed to create entry points, not barriers. Borrowers who understand this stop delaying and start evaluating real options. Cash is important, but fear about cash is often misplaced.

$4,200 to Closing: How FHA Made the Numbers Work

Jasmine believed her low credit score meant she needed a huge savings account to buy a home. Her score was 574, and she had delayed applying for over a year, assuming she needed at least $20,000 in cash. When she finally spoke with an FHA-focused lender, the math told a very different story.

Jasmine earned $4,600 per month and wanted to purchase a $230,000 home using FHA financing. Her minimum FHA down payment at 3.5 percent was $8,050. Her estimated closing costs were approximately $7,200, bringing her total initial cash requirement to $15,250.

At first glance, the number seemed overwhelming. But the lender structured the transaction strategically. The seller agreed to contribute $6,000 toward Jasmine's closing costs. Jasmine also received a documented gift of $5,000 from a family member. These two components reduced her required cash dramatically.

After applying the seller credit and gift funds, Jasmine's remaining out-of-pocket requirement dropped to $4,250. Her monthly FHA mortgage payment, including taxes, insurance, and mortgage insurance, was estimated at $1,540. Her existing debts totaled $410 per month. Adding the housing payment resulted in total obligations of $1,950. Dividing $1,950 by her $4,600 income produced a debt-to-income ratio of approximately 42.4 percent, well within FHA guidelines.

Jasmine still retained $3,800 in savings after closing, providing additional stability. Her credit score did not change. Her income did not change. The strategy changed.

Jasmine closed on her FHA loan with less cash than she had spent delaying the process. The fear was never in the numbers—it was in the assumptions.

That is the power of understanding FHA cash rules.

Chapter 9

Approved Is Just the Beginning: Using FHA to Rebuild Credit and Build Momentum

For many borrowers with low credit or past credit issues, FHA approval feels like the finish line. After years of being told no, getting approved can feel like a miracle—a moment to exhale and stop thinking about credit altogether. While that relief is understandable, FHA approval is not the end of the journey. It is the beginning of a new financial phase, one where homeownership becomes a powerful tool for rebuilding credit, strengthening stability, and creating long-term opportunity.

FHA loans are designed not only to provide access but to support recovery. Once a borrower becomes a homeowner, their monthly mortgage payment becomes the most important trade line on their credit report. A well-managed FHA mortgage can improve credit scores steadily over time, often faster than revolving credit alone. Each on-time payment reinforces a pattern of responsibility that underwriters and future lenders value highly.

One of the most immediate changes borrowers experience after closing is predictability. Rent often increases unpredictably, while mortgage payments tend to remain stable. This stability allows borrowers to plan more effectively, reduce stress, and allocate resources strategically. FHA borrowers who understand this begin to shift from survival mode into planning mode, which has lasting financial effects.

Equity accumulation is another overlooked benefit of FHA homeownership. Each mortgage payment reduces principal over time, gradually increasing ownership stake. Even modest appreciation combined with amortization can create meaningful equity within a few years. For borrowers who previously felt locked out of asset building, this shift can be transformative. FHA provides a foothold in the market that allows borrowers to participate in long-term wealth creation.

Credit behavior after closing matters as much as behavior before approval. Borrowers who continue paying all obligations on time, avoid excessive new credit, and manage revolving balances carefully often see significant score increases within the first 12 to 24 months of homeownership. FHA borrowers who treat their mortgage as a foundation rather than a finish line position themselves for refinancing opportunities, lower interest rates, and expanded financial options.

Refinancing is an important part of the FHA strategy. Many borrowers enter FHA with higher interest rates due to credit risk. Over time, improved credit and equity may allow refinancing into a lower-rate FHA streamline or even a conventional loan. FHA streamlines require minimal documentation and no appraisal in many cases, making them accessible tools for borrowers who maintain good payment history.

Homeownership also changes how borrowers are viewed by lenders, insurers, and even employers. A consistent housing payment demonstrates responsibility at a scale larger than any credit card. This perception shift opens doors beyond mortgages. Borrowers often find that other financial products become more accessible as their profile strengthens.

The emotional impact of FHA homeownership cannot be overlooked. Stability builds confidence. Confidence leads to better financial decisions. Borrowers who once felt defined by their credit past begin to redefine themselves through consistent action. FHA approval becomes proof that recovery is real and progress is measurable.

This chapter exists to encourage borrowers not to stop at approval. FHA is not a concession—it is a catalyst. When used intentionally, it becomes one of the most powerful rebuilding tools available. Homeownership is not just about having a place to live. It is about creating momentum that carries forward.

From FHA Approval to Financial Lift: The Two-Year Transformation

Carlos was approved for an FHA loan with a credit score of 568. His monthly mortgage payment, including taxes, insurance, and mortgage insurance, was $1,580 on a $240,000 home. His income was $5,200 per month, and his existing debts totaled $420. His debt-to-income ratio at closing was approximately 38.5 percent.

Over the first year, Carlos made every mortgage payment on time. His rent payment was replaced by a mortgage payment that remained stable, allowing him to budget more effectively. After 12 months, his credit score increased to 610. His income remained steady, and he reduced his revolving balances slightly.

After two years, Carlos's mortgage balance had decreased to approximately $230,000. His home's value increased modestly to $260,000. This created approximately $30,000 in equity. His credit score had risen to 640 due to consistent payment history and improved utilization.

Carlos explored refinancing options. A streamline refinance

reduced his interest rate, lowering his monthly payment by $180. His new payment became $1,400 per month. This reduction freed up $2,160 annually, which Carlos redirected toward savings and debt reduction.

The math told a powerful story. FHA approval was not the end—it was the engine. Carlos didn't wait for perfect credit. He built it through ownership.

That is the long-term power of FHA when used intentionally.

Chapter 10

From Denied to Designed: How Smart Borrowers Win with FHA on Their Own Terms

For many borrowers, the FHA journey begins with doubt. Years of rejection, misinformation, and self-blame create the belief that homeownership is something granted only to those with perfect financial histories. This belief is reinforced every time a borrower hears "your credit isn't ready" without explanation or strategy. The truth is that FHA loans were never meant to reward perfection. They were designed to reward readiness. Borrowers who understand this stop reacting to denial and start designing outcomes.

Throughout this book, one message has remained consistent: FHA approval is not accidental. It is the result of understanding how the system works and aligning behavior with that system. Borrowers with low credit or past credit issues are not excluded from FHA lending. They are often its intended beneficiaries. What separates successful borrowers from discouraged ones is not their past—it is their preparation.

FHA underwriting evaluates risk through patterns. It looks for stability in income, consistency in payments, reasonable debt levels, and thoughtful use of cash. It allows flexibility where conventional lending does not. But flexibility does not mean randomness. Borrowers who win with FHA do so by making intentional choices. They time their applications, structure their finances, select the right lenders, and present clear, credible stories.

One of the most powerful shifts borrowers can make is moving from emotional decision-making to strategic planning. Paying off old debts out of fear, applying too early, or accepting the first denial as final are emotional reactions. FHA lending rewards calm, informed action. Borrowers who pause, assess, and adjust often achieve approval faster than those who rush.

This chapter exists to help borrowers step into ownership of the process. FHA guidelines are public. The rules are knowable. Borrowers who educate themselves gain leverage. They stop feeling powerless and start asking better questions. They understand why one lender said no and another said yes. They recognize when to wait and when to move forward. Knowledge replaces anxiety.

Another key lesson is that FHA approval is not a single moment—it is a continuum. The same behaviors that lead to approval also lead to long-term success. Managing debt responsibly, protecting payment history, maintaining reserves, and budgeting sustainably do not end at closing. They compound over time, improving credit, increasing equity, and opening future opportunities.

Borrowers who approach FHA as a stepping stone rather than a concession often outperform those who wait for perfect credit. FHA allows borrowers to enter the housing market earlier, stabilize their housing costs, and rebuild credit through ownership. This forward momentum is often more valuable than waiting years to qualify for a different loan product.

It is also important to acknowledge that not every borrower will be approved immediately. FHA does not guarantee approval—but it does provide a clear path. Borrowers who are not yet ready can become ready by following the principles outlined in this book. Preparation is measurable. Readiness is achievable.

This final chapter is not about optimism alone—it is about agency. FHA lending works best when borrowers understand that they are participants, not passengers. Every financial decision tells a story. FHA underwriters read that story carefully. Borrowers who write it intentionally change outcomes.

Homeownership is not a reward for flawless credit. It is a tool for stability, growth, and recovery. FHA was built to make that tool accessible. Borrowers who understand this stop waiting for permission and start building qualification on their own terms.

This book began by challenging the idea that a credit score defines a borrower. It ends by reinforcing a stronger truth: informed borrowers define their own outcomes. FHA is not the exception—it is the opportunity.

The Same Numbers, a Different Result: FHA Success by Design

Nicole had applied for a mortgage twice before and was denied both times. Her credit score was 576, and she carried two old collections and a prior late payment history. Each denial reinforced the belief that she simply wasn't ready. When Nicole decided to try again, she did something different—she approached the process intentionally.

Nicole earned $5,000 per month and wanted to purchase a $238,000 home using FHA financing. Her estimated FHA mortgage payment, including taxes, insurance, and mortgage insurance, was $1,600 per month. Her existing debts included a $330 car payment and $95 in credit card minimums, totaling $425.

Adding the housing payment brought her total monthly

obligations to $2,025. Dividing $2,025 by her $5,000 income produced a debt-to-income ratio of approximately 40.5 percent. These numbers had been present in her previous applications as well. The difference was not the math—it was the structure.

Nicole worked with an FHA-focused lender who reviewed her full profile. Her collections were over three years old. Her late payments were over 18 months old. She had paid $1,580 in rent on time for two years. She had $7,000 in savings and would retain $5,000 after closing.

The lender structured her application carefully. No unnecessary debt was paid off. No new credit was opened. A clear explanation letter documented her past hardship and recovery. The file told a coherent story of stabilization.

The underwriter approved the loan. The same credit score that once led to denial now supported approval because the context changed. Nicole closed on her home with confidence, not surprise.

The math never changed. The borrower did.

That is how FHA success is designed—not hoped for.

Chapter 11

The Silent Killers: How Borrowers Lose FHA Approval After Doing Everything Right

One of the most painful experiences a borrower can face is losing an FHA approval after believing everything was finally on track. These situations are especially frustrating because they rarely happen due to major issues. Instead, they occur because of small, misunderstood actions that quietly change a borrower's risk profile between application and closing. For borrowers with low credit or past credit issues, this window is especially sensitive. FHA approvals are conditional by nature, and understanding how to protect that approval is just as important as earning it.

FHA underwriting evaluates borrowers at multiple stages. Initial approval does not lock the loan permanently. Underwriters continue to assess risk until closing, and changes during this period can alter the decision. Borrowers often assume that once they are "approved," they can relax. In reality, this is the moment when discipline matters most. FHA approvals are built on stability, and any disruption to that stability raises questions. One of the most common approval killers is new credit activity. Opening a credit card, financing furniture, buying a car, or even increasing balances can change debt ratios and credit scores overnight. Borrowers often justify these actions emotionally, believing small changes won't matter. FHA underwriting does not evaluate intent—it evaluates numbers and patterns. Even a modest increase in monthly obligations can push ratios beyond acceptable limits or signal renewed risk.

Employment changes are another silent threat. FHA requires income stability, and even positive changes such as promotions, job switches, or commission structures can introduce uncertainty. Borrowers sometimes change jobs thinking higher income will help, only to learn that FHA requires seasoning or averaging before income can be counted. Timing matters. Stability almost always outweighs improvement during the loan process.

Bank activity also plays a critical role. Large deposits, undocumented transfers, and unexplained cash movements can delay or derail approval. FHA underwriters must source funds used for closing to ensure they are legitimate. Borrowers who move money casually between accounts or receive cash without documentation create red flags that must be resolved before closing. Transparency matters more than convenience. Another overlooked issue is disputes and credit monitoring activity. Borrowers sometimes dispute accounts or enroll in credit repair programs during underwriting, believing they are helping their case. Disputes can suspend underwriting or require resolution before closing. FHA underwriters prefer accurate, stable credit reports over fluctuating scores. Rebuilding stops once underwriting begins.

Documentation fatigue is another silent killer. Borrowers may become less responsive after approval, assuming the hard part is over. FHA underwriting requires timely documentation, and delays can push files past rate locks or contract deadlines. Consistent communication is part of maintaining approval.

The emotional component of this phase cannot be ignored. Borrowers who have fought hard to qualify may feel entitled to relax. FHA underwriting does not reward entitlement—it rewards consistency. Protecting approval requires discipline, patience, and trust in the process.

This chapter exists to protect borrowers from self-sabotage. FHA approvals are fragile not because they are unfair, but because they are precise. Borrowers who understand this stop asking "Can I do this?" and start asking "Should I wait?" That awareness preserves outcomes. FHA loans are not lost because borrowers are unworthy. They are lost because borrowers underestimate the importance of stability. Approval is not just earned—it must be protected.

Approved on Paper, Denied in Practice: A $150 Mistake

Brian was approved for an FHA loan with a credit score of 581. His income was $5,600 per month, and his estimated FHA mortgage payment was $1,700. His existing debts included a $360 car payment and $120 in credit card minimums, totaling $480. His debt-to-income ratio at approval was approximately 39.6 percent.

Brian was thrilled. For the first time, homeownership felt real. While waiting for closing, he decided to finance a new living room set, adding a $150 monthly payment. He assumed the amount was small enough to be irrelevant.

When the underwriter performed a final credit refresh before closing, the new account appeared. Brian's total monthly debts increased to $630. Adding the FHA payment brought his total obligations to $2,330. Dividing $2,330 by his $5,600 income produced a new debt-to-income ratio of approximately 41.6 percent.

On its own, the ratio was still within FHA limits. However, Brian had minimal reserves and recent credit recovery. The new debt shifted his risk profile. The underwriter requested additional documentation, explanations, and compensating factors. None existed.

The loan was denied.

The numbers didn't explode. They drifted just enough to matter. A $150 decision undone months of preparation.

Brian reapplied later and was approved after reestablishing stability. The lesson stayed with him. FHA approval is not protected by excitement—it is protected by discipline.

That is how approvals are lost quietly—and how they are preserved by those who understand the rules.

Chapter 12

Your FHA Game Plan: Turning Knowledge Into a Confident Yes

By the time a borrower reaches this chapter, something important has already changed. FHA is no longer a mystery, credit is no longer a verdict, and approval is no longer something that feels random or out of reach. What remains is execution. Knowledge without action produces frustration, but knowledge paired with a plan produces results. FHA loans reward borrowers who move deliberately, not emotionally, and this chapter exists to help borrowers translate understanding into approval.

The most successful FHA borrowers approach the process like a project, not a plea. They stop asking whether they are "good enough" and start evaluating whether their profile is aligned. Alignment is measurable. It shows up in recent payment history, manageable debt, stable income, sufficient cash, and calm financial behavior. Borrowers who focus on alignment rarely feel surprised by underwriting outcomes because they have already assessed their readiness.

A strong FHA game plan begins with timing. Applying too early is one of the most common mistakes borrowers make.

FHA guidelines allow flexibility, but timing determines how that flexibility is applied. Borrowers who wait until their recent credit behavior reflects consistency give underwriters confidence. This does not require years of waiting. In many cases, three to six months of intentional behavior makes the difference between hesitation and approval.

Income planning is another core component of execution. Borrowers who understand how FHA averages income, evaluates stability, and treats overtime or variable pay are better prepared to document earnings correctly. Stability often matters more than growth. A borrower who earns slightly less but consistently is often stronger than one whose income is higher but volatile. FHA underwriting values predictability.

Debt planning completes the picture. Successful borrowers do not eliminate all debt—they structure it. They understand which debts matter, which do not, and how payments affect ratios. They avoid reactive decisions such as paying off old collections unnecessarily or opening new credit to chase scores. FHA rewards calm debt profiles, not aggressive cleanup.

Cash strategy is equally important. Borrowers who plan for down payment sources, seller credits, gift funds, and reserves remove uncertainty from the process. FHA allows multiple pathways to closing, and borrowers who understand those pathways avoid over-saving or under-preparing. Cash should be positioned intentionally, not emotionally.

Lender selection ties everything together. Even the strongest borrower profile can be misjudged by the wrong lender. Borrowers who choose FHA-experienced lenders, understand overlays, and communicate openly position themselves for smoother approvals. The right lender does not change the rules—they apply them correctly.

Perhaps the most important shift borrowers make at this stage is psychological. FHA success requires confidence without complacency. Borrowers who believe they are capable tend to act with discipline. They respond quickly to documentation requests, avoid unnecessary financial changes, and protect their approval until closing. Confidence produces consistency, and consistency produces results.

This chapter exists to close the gap between understanding and ownership. FHA lending is not about hoping underwriters are generous. It is about presenting a profile that makes approval the logical outcome. Borrowers who follow a clear game plan remove uncertainty from the equation.

Approval is not something that happens to borrowers. It is something borrowers prepare for. FHA makes that preparation accessible. When borrowers execute intentionally, the system works exactly as designed.

No Guessing, Just Math: An FHA Plan That Worked

Stephanie had spent years assuming she wasn't ready to buy. Her credit score was 572, and she had two old collections and a history of late payments from a period of unemployment. Instead of applying immediately, Stephanie decided to build a clear FHA game plan.

Stephanie earned $4,850 per month and paid $1,550 in rent. Her existing debts included a $295 car payment and $105 in credit card minimums, totaling $400. She wanted to purchase a $232,000 home using FHA financing. Her estimated FHA mortgage payment, including taxes, insurance, and mortgage insurance, was $1,560.

Before applying, Stephanie focused on execution. She made every payment on time for six months. She avoided new credit. She reduced her credit card balances slightly, lowering her minimum payments to $80. Her total monthly debts dropped to $375.

At application, Stephanie's total monthly obligations with the FHA payment were $1,935. Dividing $1,935 by her $4,850 income resulted in a debt-to-income ratio of approximately

39.9 percent. Her ratios worked cleanly. Stephanie structured her cash strategically. Her FHA down payment of 3.5 percent was $8,120. The seller agreed to contribute $5,500 toward closing costs. Stephanie received a $3,000 documented gift from a family member. Her required cash to close dropped to just under $4,000, and she retained $4,500 in reserves after closing.

The underwriter reviewed Stephanie's file. Her collections were over three years old. Her recent credit was clean. Her rent history matched her new housing payment. Her income was stable. The math aligned with the story.

Stephanie was approved without conditions beyond standard documentation. There were no surprises because nothing was left to chance. She didn't guess her way into approval—she planned her way into it.

That is the FHA game plan in action.

Chapter 13

The Underwriter's Eye: How Your FHA File Is Really Read—and Why Clarity Wins

By the time a borrower reaches this stage in the FHA process, most of the technical work has already been done. Income has been calculated, debts reviewed, credit analyzed, and ratios measured. Yet approvals and denials are still issued at this point, often leaving borrowers confused about why files that "look fine" on paper stall or fail. The missing piece is rarely math alone. It is clarity. FHA underwriting is not just an exercise in calculation—it is an exercise in interpretation.

Underwriters do not review files in a vacuum. They are tasked with assessing risk quickly, accurately, and consistently. A clean FHA file tells a clear story with minimal friction. A messy file, even when technically eligible, creates hesitation. This is especially important for borrowers with low credit or past credit issues, because their files already require more contextual review. The easier that context is to understand, the more likely approval becomes.

One of the most important concepts borrowers rarely hear is that underwriters read files horizontally, not vertically. They are not focused on one number at a time. They are looking for consistency across income, credit, assets, and behavior. When one area contradicts another, questions arise. When everything aligns, approval feels logical. Clarity reduces perceived risk.

Documentation quality plays a critical role in this process. FHA underwriting allows explanations for credit events, but explanations must make sense. Vague letters, emotional language, or excessive detail often weaken a file rather than strengthen it. Underwriters are not looking for apologies. They are looking for cause, resolution, and evidence of stability. A concise explanation paired with documented recovery is far more effective than a long narrative without structure.

Another overlooked factor is organization. A borrower may meet FHA guidelines perfectly, but if documents are incomplete, inconsistent, or difficult to verify, the file becomes burdensome. Underwriters are human. A file that requires excessive follow-up introduces friction, and friction increases perceived risk. Clean files move faster and face fewer questions.

Consistency across documents is equally important. Income shown on pay stubs must align with bank deposits. Rent history must align with bank statements or verification letters.

Assets must be traceable. FHA underwriting is designed to prevent fraud and misrepresentation, and inconsistencies—even innocent ones—trigger scrutiny. Borrowers who understand this focus on alignment, not just eligibility.

Timing also affects how a file is perceived. Last-minute document changes, sudden deposits, or rushed explanations raise concerns that otherwise would not exist. FHA underwriting rewards predictability. Borrowers who prepare documents early and maintain stability throughout the process create confidence. Confidence accelerates approval.

The emotional trap many borrowers fall into is assuming that approval is about being persuasive. It is not. Underwriters are not convinced by optimism. They are convinced by order. When a file reads cleanly from start to finish, approval becomes the natural conclusion. When it feels chaotic, even strong numbers may be questioned.

This chapter exists to help borrowers understand that FHA approval is not only about qualifying—it is about communicating qualification clearly. Borrowers who take ownership of how their file is presented remove unnecessary obstacles. They do not rely on underwriters to "figure it out." They make it obvious.

Clarity is one of the most powerful compensating factors available. It does not cost money, raise credit scores, or require waiting. It simply requires intention. Borrowers who understand how underwriters read files stop fearing the process and start respecting it. That respect shows up in results.

Same Numbers, Cleaner Story: The Approval That Came Easily

Monica had already been told no once. Her credit score was 578, her income was steady at $5,200 per month, and her debts were manageable. The denial left her confused because the math seemed to work. When she applied again, nothing about her financial profile changed—but everything about her presentation did.

Monica wanted to purchase a $240,000 home using FHA financing. Her estimated FHA mortgage payment, including taxes, insurance, and mortgage insurance, was $1,600 per month. Her existing debts included a $340 car payment and $110 in credit card minimums, totaling $450.

Adding the housing payment resulted in total monthly obligations of $2,050. Dividing $2,050 by her $5,200 income produced a debt-to-income ratio of approximately 39.4 percent. These were the same numbers from her prior denial.

The difference was structure. Monica worked with a lender who organized her file carefully. Her rent history of $1,575 per month for two years was documented clearly. Her bank statements matched her income deposits exactly. Her old collections were over three years old and left untouched. Her letter of explanation was brief, factual, and documented recovery.

The underwriter reviewed the file without hesitation. There were no inconsistencies to resolve, no missing links to question. The numbers aligned with the story, and the story aligned with the documents.

Monica was approved quickly and with minimal conditions. Nothing about her credit score improved. Nothing about her income changed. What changed was clarity.

That is how FHA files are won—not by changing the math, but by making the math easy to believe.

Chapter 14

After the Keys: How to Protect Your FHA Win and Turn Approval Into Leverage

For many borrowers, closing day feels like the end of a long and exhausting journey. The paperwork is signed, the keys are handed over, and the pressure finally lifts. For borrowers who fought through low credit, past mistakes, and repeated denials, the moment can feel surreal. Yet in the FHA world, closing is not the finish line. It is the transition point between qualification and leverage. What borrowers do after closing determines whether FHA becomes a one-time victory or a long-term advantage.

The first year of homeownership is especially important for borrowers who entered FHA with credit challenges. The mortgage payment immediately becomes the largest and most influential trade line on the credit report. Each on-time payment reinforces a pattern of stability that underwriters value far more than short-term score increases. FHA borrowers who protect this payment above all else often see measurable credit improvement without aggressive rebuilding tactics. One of the most common mistakes borrowers make after closing is relaxing financial discipline too quickly. The excitement of homeownership can lead to new furniture purchases, credit card usage, or vehicle upgrades. While these decisions may feel justified, they can slow or reverse the very progress FHA made possible. Borrowers who treat the first 12 months as a stabilization phase rather than a spending phase protect their momentum.

Budgeting takes on new meaning after closing. Mortgage payments introduce predictability, but they also demand consistency. FHA borrowers who align their budgets around housing first tend to experience lower stress and better outcomes. The goal is not restriction—it is control. Control creates flexibility later.

Another key element of protecting an FHA win is understanding equity growth. Even in the early years, each payment reduces principal. Combined with modest appreciation, equity begins forming quietly. Borrowers who track this progress gain perspective. FHA is not just a loan—it is an entry point into ownership. Ownership changes how time works in your favor.

Refinancing strategy is also part of the post-closing mindset. FHA borrowers who improve credit and maintain strong payment history often qualify for streamline refinances or transitions into conventional loans sooner than expected. These options are not automatic—they are earned through consistency. Borrowers who understand this treat each payment as an investment rather than an obligation.

Credit behavior outside the mortgage matters as well. Keeping revolving balances low, avoiding unnecessary new accounts, and maintaining emergency savings strengthen the profile continuously. FHA borrowers who behave as if underwriting never ends tend to outperform those who assume approval granted immunity.

Emotionally, post-closing discipline can be challenging. Borrowers may feel they have proven themselves and deserve to enjoy the reward. The truth is that enjoyment grows when stability compounds. FHA lending opens the door, but behavior determines how far that door stays open.

This chapter exists to help borrowers avoid the trap of short-term thinking. FHA approval is not fragile if protected intentionally. Borrowers who understand how to preserve and build upon their success turn homeownership into leverage rather than pressure.

Closing gives you keys. What you do next builds control.

One Payment at a Time: How FHA Turned Stability Into Opportunity

Andre closed on his FHA loan with a credit score of 574. His mortgage payment, including taxes, insurance, and mortgage insurance, was $1,620 per month on a $245,000 home. His income was $5,400 per month, and his remaining debts totaled $420. His debt-to-income ratio at closing was approximately 37.8 percent.

During his first year of homeownership, Andre made every payment on time. He resisted financing new furniture and avoided opening new credit accounts. Instead, he kept his revolving balances low and built a small emergency fund. After 12 months, his credit score increased to 612, largely due to the positive mortgage payment history.

After two years, Andre's loan balance dropped to approximately $235,000. His home's value increased modestly to $265,000. This created roughly $30,000 in equity. His credit score reached 638, and his overall debt decreased slightly as balances were paid down.

Andre explored refinancing options. A streamline refinance reduced his interest rate, lowering his monthly payment by $160. His new payment became $1,460. Over a year, this saved $1,920. Over five years, it totaled $9,600—money that Andre redirected toward savings and future investments.

Andre didn't change jobs. He didn't dramatically increase income. He didn't chase credit hacks. He protected what FHA gave him and let time do the work.

That is how FHA wins are protected—and how they grow.

Chapter 15

From Borrower to Owner: The Moment You Stop Asking for Permission

There is a quiet moment that happens for many FHA borrowers after everything settles. The loan is closed, the payments are steady, the credit score is rising, and the fear that once dominated every financial decision begins to fade. It is the moment when a borrower realizes they are no longer trying to qualify for something—they are managing something they own. This shift is subtle, but it is profound. FHA does not just help people buy homes. It helps them change how they see themselves financially.

Borrowers with low credit or past credit issues often spend years operating from a defensive mindset. Every decision feels reactive. Every bill feels like a threat. Every denial reinforces the belief that systems are designed to keep them out. FHA interrupts that cycle. It provides structure, predictability, and proof that recovery is possible. But the real transformation happens when borrowers stop viewing FHA as a rescue and start viewing it as a foundation.

Ownership changes behavior. When a borrower becomes a homeowner, their decisions begin to carry long-term weight.

Payments are no longer temporary. Credit behavior is no longer abstract. Equity becomes visible. FHA borrowers who embrace this shift begin thinking differently about money, timing, and risk. They stop asking whether they "can" and start deciding whether they "should."

This chapter exists to help borrowers recognize that point of transition. FHA was designed to be accessible, but it was never meant to trap borrowers in limitation. It is a starting place, not a ceiling. Borrowers who understand FHA deeply often become some of the most disciplined homeowners because they remember what instability felt like. That memory becomes a strength.

Financial confidence does not come from perfect credit scores. It comes from predictability. Predictability comes from habits. FHA borrowers who maintain consistent payment behavior, protect their cash flow, and avoid unnecessary financial shocks begin to operate with clarity instead of fear. They do not chase every opportunity. They evaluate them.

Another critical evolution happens in how borrowers interact with lenders. Early in the process, borrowers often feel intimidated by underwriting. Later, they understand it. They ask informed questions. They recognize when guidance is sound and when it is overly conservative. They stop assuming authority equals accuracy. This confidence is earned, not granted.

Wealth-building does not require dramatic leaps. It requires sustained alignment. FHA borrowers who remain disciplined often find themselves eligible for refinancing, improved terms, or alternative loan products sooner than expected. The same behaviors that created approval now create choice. Choice is the real milestone.

This chapter is not about encouraging risk. It is about encouraging ownership—of decisions, outcomes, and direction. FHA gives borrowers a seat at the table. What they do with that seat determines the long-term result.

Borrowers who complete this journey stop defining themselves by where they started. They define themselves by how they operate now. FHA was the door. Ownership is the room. Control is the goal.

This is where fear ends—not because risk disappears, but because understanding replaces it.

The Shift Nobody Talks About: When FHA Stops Feeling Like FHA

Derrick closed on his FHA loan with a credit score of 569. His mortgage payment, including taxes, insurance, and mortgage insurance, was $1,580 per month on a $238,000 home. His income was $5,300 per month, and his remaining debts totaled $390. At closing, his debt-to-income ratio was approximately 37.2 percent.

During his first two years of homeownership, Derrick treated his mortgage as non-negotiable. He paid every payment on time and avoided unnecessary credit. His credit score rose to 615 after one year and 642 after two years. His loan balance dropped to approximately $228,000, while his home's value increased to $265,000. This created roughly $37,000 in equity.

In year three, Derrick refinanced out of FHA into a conventional loan. His new interest rate reduced his monthly payment by $190, bringing it down to $1,390. Over a year, this saved $2,280. Over five years, it would save $11,400.

But the most important change wasn't in the numbers. Derrick no longer felt anxious when reviewing financial decisions. He understood how lenders evaluated risk. He knew how to protect his profile. He made decisions intentionally instead of emotionally.

The FHA loan that once felt like a lifeline became just another chapter in a larger story. Derrick didn't outgrow FHA because his credit became perfect. He outgrew it because his habits did.

That is the moment borrowers stop asking for permission—and start operating with confidence.

Final Thoughts

If there is one idea this book was written to replace, it is the belief that credit history is destiny. Too many capable, responsible people spend years believing they are disqualified from homeownership because of numbers that reflect their past rather than their present. FHA loans exist because that belief is incomplete. They were created to recognize recovery, stability, and forward progress. This book was written to help you see yourself not as a risk to be judged, but as a borrower to be understood.

Throughout these chapters, you have seen that FHA lending is not about perfection. It is about patterns. It is about recent behavior, consistent income, manageable obligations, and thoughtful preparation. Borrowers with late payments, collections, charge-offs, bankruptcies, or low credit scores are not automatically excluded from FHA financing. In many cases, they are the very borrowers FHA was designed to serve. What matters is not where you started, but how you have responded.

One of the most important lessons in this book is that denial is not always a reflection of eligibility. Often, it is a reflection of misunderstanding—by borrowers, lenders, or both. FHA guidelines are flexible, but they are not random. When borrowers understand how those guidelines are applied, approval becomes less mysterious and far more predictable. Knowledge transforms the process from something that happens to you into something you actively participate in.

This book has shown you that timing matters. Recent credit behavior carries more weight than old mistakes. Stability matters more than speed. Calm financial patterns matter more than dramatic cleanups. Borrowers who rush often stumble, while borrowers who plan often succeed. FHA does not reward urgency—it rewards readiness.

You have also learned that structure matters. Debt is not the enemy; imbalance is. Cash is not a punishment; it is a tool. Credit rebuilding is not about chasing scores; it is about demonstrating control. The most successful FHA borrowers are not those with the highest scores, but those whose financial picture makes sense when viewed as a whole.

Perhaps most importantly, this book has emphasized that lender choice matters. FHA is a federal program, but its application varies widely. A denial from one lender does not define your eligibility. Borrowers who learn to distinguish between FHA guidelines and lender overlays stop internalizing rejection and start navigating strategically. This shift alone changes outcomes. If you are walking away from this book with a clearer understanding of how FHA underwriting actually works, then it has done its job. But understanding is only the first step. The true value of this knowledge is in how you apply it. FHA lending rewards intentional behavior over time. Small decisions, made consistently, often matter more than large, reactive changes.

Homeownership is not a finish line. It is a platform. FHA loans are not concessions; they are entry points. For borrowers who use them wisely, they become tools for rebuilding credit, stabilizing housing costs, accumulating equity, and opening future opportunities. Many borrowers who once believed FHA was their only option later discover that it was their gateway to choice.

It is also important to acknowledge that not every borrower will be approved immediately. That reality does not mean failure. FHA provides a path, not a promise. Readiness can be built. Stability can be demonstrated. Time can work in your favor when guided intentionally. Borrowers who are not approved today are often far closer than they think.

The emotional weight of credit should not be underestimated. Shame, fear, and self-doubt often do more damage than the credit report itself. FHA lending was never meant to reinforce those feelings. It was meant to create access. Borrowers who release shame and replace it with strategy move differently. They ask better questions. They make better decisions. They stop hiding and start preparing.

As you move forward, remember this: underwriters are not looking for perfect people. They are looking for predictable outcomes. When your financial story shows recovery, consistency, and responsibility, approval becomes logical rather than generous. FHA works best when it is understood, respected, and used intentionally.

This book began with the idea that your credit score is not your story. It ends with a stronger truth: your actions are. FHA loans give borrowers the opportunity to rewrite their financial narrative—not overnight, but meaningfully. When used correctly, they turn "almost" into "approved," and "approved" into "secure."

Homeownership is not reserved for the flawless. It is built by the prepared.

That is the real promise of FHA—and the real takeaway of this book.

The FHA Homeownership & Wealth Series

Complete Roadmap: From First-Time Buyer to Long-Term Wealth Builder

The FHA Homeownership & Wealth Series is designed as a progressive journey. Each book builds on the previous one, guiding borrowers from basic understanding to confident ownership, strategic financing, and long-term wealth creation. Readers can enter at any stage, but those who follow the full roadmap gain the clearest, fastest path to results.

This series is structured to meet borrowers exactly where they are—and show them what comes next.

Phase 1: Foundation & Confidence (Books 1–3)

Understanding FHA and realizing you qualify

These books eliminate confusion, fear, and misinformation. They are designed to answer the most important early question: *Is homeownership actually possible for me?*

Book 1 – FHA Loans Explained for Beginners How FHA Mortgages Work, Who Qualifies, and Why They're One of the Easiest Paths to Homeownership This is the foundation of the entire series. Readers learn how FHA loans work, why they exist, and how to evaluate FHA realistically using math instead of myths. This book builds confidence and replaces hesitation with clarity.

Book 2 – Buying Your First Home with FHA A Step-by-Step Guide to Purchasing a Home with Low Down Payment and Flexible Credit Rules This book turns understanding into action. Readers learn the full buying process—from pre-approval to closing—so they know exactly what to expect and how to avoid common first-time buyer mistakes.

Book 3 – FHA Loans for Borrowers with Low Credit or Past Credit Issues How to Get Approved with FHA Even with Late Payments, Collections, or a Low Credit Score This book is for borrowers who believe their credit disqualifies them. It explains FHA's second-chance philosophy and shows how recovery, not perfection, determines approval.

Phase 2: Income Reality & Property Flexibility (Books 4–6)

Qualifying with real-life finances and real homes

These books expand what readers believe is possible by addressing income types, property types, and cash requirements.

Book 4 – FHA Loans for Self-Employed, 1099 & Gig Workers How Business Owners and Independent

Contractors Qualify for FHA Home Loans This book demystifies income calculations for non-traditional earners and shows how FHA accommodates modern work patterns.

Book 5 – FHA Loans for Fixer-Uppers, Condos & Non-Perfect Homes How to Buy Homes That Need Repairs or Don't Fit Traditional Loan Guidelines Readers learn how FHA views property condition and how renovation and condo options expand buying opportunities.

Book 6 – FHA Loan Limits, Down Payment & Closing Costs How Much You Can Borrow and How to Bring Less Money to the Closing Table This book focuses on numbers. Readers learn how FHA loan limits work, how to reduce cash to close, and how seller credits and assistance programs change affordability.

Phase 3: Optimization & Refinancing Strategy (Books 7–8)

Using FHA beyond the purchase

These books show how FHA loans evolve with the borrower.

Book 7 – FHA Refinance Options Made Simple Streamline, Rate-and-Term, and Cash-Out Refinancing Explained for Homeowners Readers learn how FHA supports refinancing, payment reduction, and financial repositioning over time.

Book 8 – Using an FHA Cash-Out Refinance to Build Wealth How to Turn Home Equity into Cash Without Selling Your Home This book introduces equity as a strategic tool, not just a number on paper, while emphasizing responsible use.

Phase 4: Income & Expansion (Books 9–10)

Turning ownership into leverage

These books shift the reader from homeowner to strategist.

Book 9 – Buying Multi-Unit Homes with FHA How to Purchase 2–4 Unit Properties, Live in One, and Rent the Rest Readers learn how FHA enables owner-occupied investing and rent-offset strategies that dramatically reduce housing costs.

Book 10 – FHA Loan Myths, Mistakes & Borrower Strategies What Most Buyers Get Wrong—and How Smart Borrowers Win with FHA Loans This is the strategic wrap-up book that reinforces best practices, avoids costly errors, and helps readers think like informed borrowers.

About the Author

Joe Correa is a mortgage professional, educator, and financial strategist dedicated to helping everyday people understand homeownership, credit, and wealth-building without confusion or intimidation. With years of hands-on experience in the mortgage industry, Joe has worked with first-time buyers, self-employed borrowers, credit-challenged families, and aspiring investors who were often told "no" before learning what was actually possible.

What sets Joe apart is his ability to translate complex lending rules into clear, practical guidance. Rather than relying on theory, his work is grounded in real-world scenarios, real numbers, and real borrower outcomes. He believes that most people do not fail to buy homes because they lack income or discipline, but because they lack accurate information. His mission is to replace myths with math and fear with understanding.

Joe specializes in FHA loans because he has seen firsthand how transformative they can be when used correctly. He views FHA not as a last resort, but as one of the most powerful entry points into homeownership and long-term wealth—especially for borrowers navigating modern financial realities such as student loans, variable income, credit recovery, or limited savings. Through his writing, Joe teaches borrowers how to think strategically, act confidently, and use lending tools intentionally rather than emotionally.

In addition to his mortgage work, Joe is the creator of multiple educational programs and book series focused on homeownership, credit building, refinancing strategies, and financial independence. His approach emphasizes sustainability over speculation and progress over perfection. He is known for breaking down decisions into simple frameworks that empower readers to make smart choices at every stage of their journey.

Joe's writing style reflects his core belief: financial education should be accessible, practical, and empowering. He does not promise shortcuts or hype outcomes. Instead, he provides clarity, structure, and realistic paths forward—so readers can move from uncertainty to ownership with confidence.

When he is not writing or working with borrowers, Joe continues developing educational resources designed to help families build stability, equity, and long-term opportunity through informed financial decisions.

How to Get a Personalized FHA Review

If you found this book helpful, you may want to see how FHA loan options apply to your specific income, credit profile, cash to close, and homeownership goals.

Every borrower's situation is different. FHA guidelines, loan limits, interest rates, mortgage insurance, and available options vary based on income type, credit history, debt levels, savings, property type, and state guidelines. The examples in this book are educational, but your personal FHA eligibility, payment range, and strategy can only be determined through an individualized review.

As a licensed mortgage broker, I offer a **Personalized FHA Review** designed to show you: • Whether you currently qualify for an FHA loan • Your realistic home price and monthly payment range • How much cash you may need for down payment and closing costs • How credit, debt, or income factors affect your approval • Whether FHA is the best option for you now or later • What steps, if any, would strengthen your position

This review is fast, confidential, and focused entirely on helping you make informed homeownership decisions—without pressure or obligation.

To request your personalized FHA review, visit:https://finibimortgage.carrd.co/

You may also submit your information through the QR code provided in this book.

Your financial profile already tells a story.This review shows you how FHA lenders will read it.

Yours truly,

Joseph G. Correa

Licensed Mortgage Broker, Finibi Mortgage

Educational & Financial Disclaimer

This book is provided for educational and informational purposes only. The content is intended to help readers better understand FHA loans, homeownership concepts, and general mortgage strategies, but it does not constitute financial advice, legal advice, tax advice, or lending approval. Mortgage guidelines, FHA requirements, interest rates, loan programs, and qualification standards are subject to change and may vary based on individual circumstances, lender overlays, geographic location, and market conditions.

Nothing in this book should be interpreted as a guarantee of loan approval, loan terms, interest rates, or eligibility. All examples, scenarios, calculations, and illustrations are for educational purposes only and are not intended to represent actual loan offers or outcomes. Individual results will vary based on credit profile, income stability, debt obligations, assets, property characteristics, and lender-specific requirements.

Readers are encouraged to consult with a licensed mortgage professional, financial advisor, tax professional, or legal advisor before making any financial or real estate decisions. This book does not replace personalized advice or professional review. Any decisions made based on the information in this book are the sole responsibility of the reader.

The author and publisher are not responsible for any actions taken by readers as a result of the information provided in this book. While every effort has been made to ensure accuracy at the time of publication, no representation or warranty is made regarding the completeness, reliability, or current applicability of the information contained herein.

By reading this book, you acknowledge that homeownership and mortgage decisions involve risk and personal responsibility, and you agree that the author and publisher are not liable for any financial outcomes, losses, or damages that may result from reliance on this material.

This book is designed to educate, not to instruct or advise on individual financial decisions. Its purpose is to provide general understanding so readers can ask better questions, seek appropriate professional guidance, and make informed choices based on their unique circumstances.

Risk Disclosure

Homeownership and mortgage financing involve financial risk. While FHA loans are designed to increase access to homeownership and provide flexible qualification standards, they do not eliminate risk, and outcomes may vary based on individual circumstances, market conditions, and personal financial decisions. Purchasing or refinancing a home requires a long-term financial commitment and should be evaluated carefully.

Housing markets can fluctuate. Property values may increase or decrease over time, and there is no guarantee that a home will appreciate in value. Economic conditions, interest rate changes, local market factors, and unforeseen events can affect property values, mortgage payments, and resale opportunities. Borrowers should be prepared for the possibility that home values may remain flat or decline during certain periods.

Mortgage payments represent a fixed obligation that must be met regardless of changes in income, employment status, health, or personal circumstances. Failure to make mortgage payments may result in late fees, credit damage, default, or foreclosure. Borrowers should ensure they have adequate income stability, savings, and contingency planning before entering into any mortgage obligation.

FHA loans include mortgage insurance, which increases the total cost of borrowing. While mortgage insurance enables access to lower down payments and more flexible credit standards, it may remain in place for a significant portion of the loan term unless refinanced or otherwise removed under applicable guidelines. Borrowers should understand how mortgage insurance affects monthly payments and long-term costs.

Refinancing, selling, or leveraging home equity is not guaranteed to be available in the future. These options depend on market conditions, interest rates, credit profile, equity levels, and lender requirements at the time of action. Borrowers should not assume future refinancing opportunities or equity access when making initial homeownership decisions.

Rental income, including income from multi-unit properties or converted rentals, is not guaranteed. Vacancies, maintenance costs, market conditions, tenant behavior, and regulatory changes can impact rental cash flow. Borrowers considering rental strategies should evaluate these risks carefully and avoid relying on projected rental income for financial stability.

This book does not provide investment advice or predict financial outcomes. All examples and scenarios are illustrative only and should not be relied upon as forecasts or guarantees. Readers are responsible for conducting their own due diligence and seeking professional advice when appropriate.

By choosing to pursue homeownership or mortgage financing, readers acknowledge the presence of risk and accept responsibility for their financial decisions. The author and publisher are not responsible for any losses, damages, or adverse outcomes resulting from actions taken based on the information provided in this book.

This disclosure is intended to promote informed decision-making, not discourage homeownership. Understanding risk is a critical part of using FHA loans responsibly and sustainably.

www.ingramcontent.com/pod-product-compliance
Ingram Content Group UK Ltd.
Pitfield, Milton Keynes, MK11 3LW, UK
UKHW020158290926
15471UKWH00005B/937

9 798295 619892